Ron in the Mud
and
Ted and the Duck

PHASE 2
/ck/e/
u/r/h/

Level 1 – Pink

BookLife

Helpful Hints for Reading at Home

The graphemes (written letters) and phonemes (units of sound) used throughout this series are aligned with Letters and Sounds. This offers a consistent approach to learning whether reading at home or in the classroom.

HERE IS A LIST OF PHONEMES FOR THIS PHASE OF LEARNING. AN EXAMPLE OF THE PRONUNCIATION CAN BE FOUND IN BRACKETS.

Phase 2			
s (sat)	a (cat)	t (tap)	p (tap)
i (pin)	n (net)	m (man)	d (dog)
g (go)	o (sock)	c (cat)	k (kin)
ck (sack)	e (elf)	u (up)	r (rabbit)
h (hut)	b (ball)	f (fish)	ff (off)
l (lip)	ll (ball)	ss (hiss)	

HERE ARE SOME WORDS WHICH YOUR CHILD MAY FIND TRICKY.

Phase 2 Tricky Words			
the	to	I	no
go	into		

GPC focus: /ck/e/u/r/h/

TOP TIPS FOR HELPING YOUR CHILD TO READ:

• Allow children time to break down unfamiliar words into units of sound and then encourage children to string these sounds together to create the word.

• Encourage your child to point out any focus phonics when they are used.

• Read through the book more than once to grow confidence.

• Ask simple questions about the text to assess understanding.

• Encourage children to use illustrations as prompts.

PHASE 2
/ck/e/
u/r/h/

This book focuses on the phonemes /ck/, /e/, /u/, /r/ and /h/ and is a pink level 1 book band.

Ron in the Mud

and

Ted and the Duck

Written by
Rachel Seretny

Illustrated by
Richard Bayley

RON

Can you say this sound and draw it with your finger?

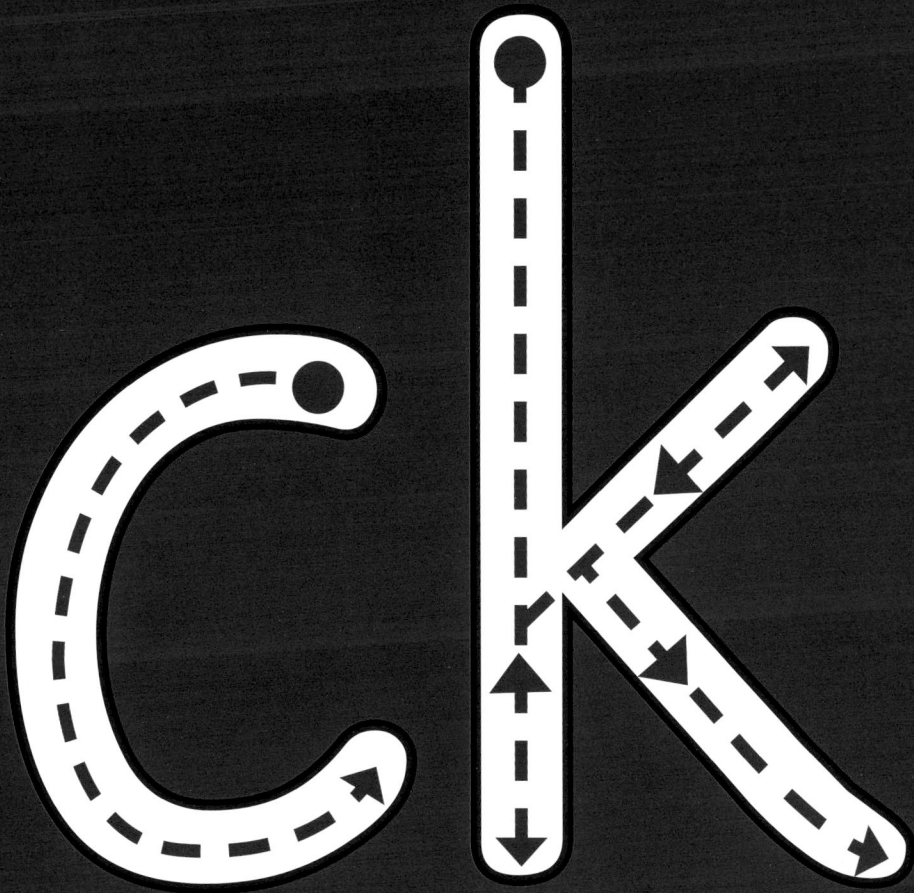

c k

Ron in the Mud

Written by
Rachel Seretny

Illustrated by
Richard Bayley

Meg is a pig.

The mud in the pen.

Meg is in the mud.

Ron is a pet pug.

Ron can run in the mud.

Meg is sad. Is Ron sad?

The sun is hot.

The mud has set!

I am Rick!

Peck, peck, peck.

Ron can run!

Meg and Ron in the mud.

Can you say this sound and draw it with your finger?

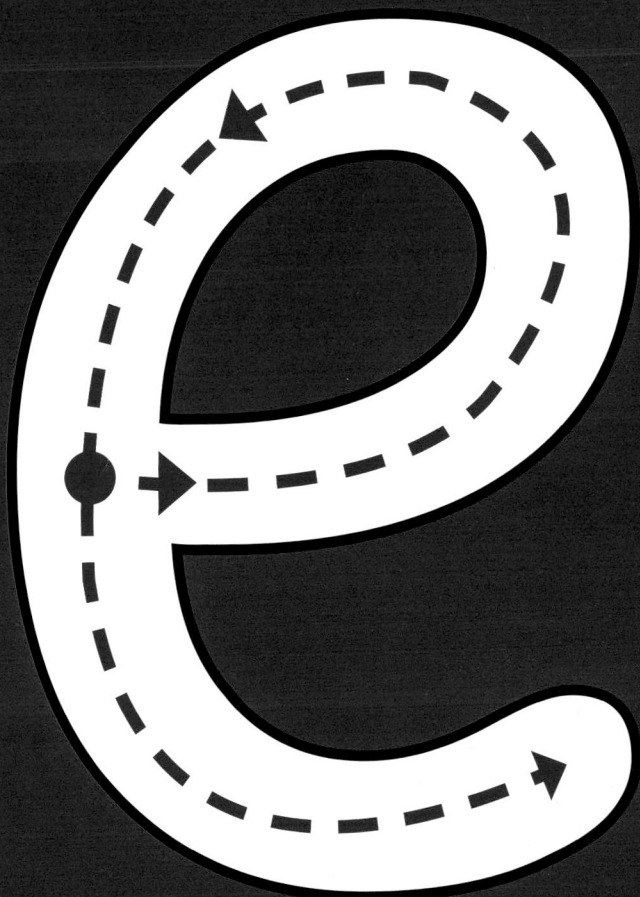

Ted and the Duck

Written by
Rachel Seretny

Illustrated by
Richard Bayley

"Go up it, Ted."

Ted is at the top.

It is a mud den.

Ted is in the mud den.

A man and a duck nap.

Ted has the duck.

The man is mad!

Run, run, run!

Run to Mum.

The duck sat.

Ted and Mum get an egg.

BookLife PUBLISHING

BookLife Readers

©2021 **BookLife Publishing Ltd.**
King's Lynn, Norfolk PE30 4LS

ISBN 978–1–83927–422–0

Ron in the Mud & Ted and the Duck
Written by Rachel Seretny
Illustrated by Richard Bayley

An Introduction to BookLife Readers...

Our Readers have been specifically created in line with the London Institute of Education's approach to book banding and are phonetically decodable and ordered to support each phase of Letters and Sounds.

Each book has been created to provide the best possible reading and learning experience. Our aim is to share our love of books with children, providing both emerging readers and prolific page–turners with beautiful books that are guaranteed to provoke interest and learning, regardless of ability.

BOOK BAND GRADED using the Institute of Education's approach to levelling.

PHONETICALLY DECODABLE supporting each phase of Letters and Sounds.

EXERCISES AND QUESTIONS to offer reinforcement and to ascertain comprehension.

BEAUTIFULLY ILLUSTRATED to inspire and provoke engagement, providing a variety of styles for the reader to enjoy whilst reading through the series.

AUTHOR INSIGHT:
RACHEL SERETNY

Rachel Seretny is a new and upcoming author for BookLife Publishing. She studied at the University of Sunderland before graduating with a PGCE from the University of East Anglia. Rachel lives in Norfolk and works as a primary school teacher. Her inspiration for writing comes from the magical imaginations of her daughter and the amazing children that she's taught.

PHASE 2
/ck/e/ u/r/h/

This book focuses on the phonemes /ck/, /e/, /u/, /r/ and /h/ and is a pink level 1 book band.